Sharks

Kate Riggs

SCHOLASTIC INC.

ISBN 978-0-545-82948-9

12 11 10 9 8 7 6 5 4 3 2 1   15 16 17 18 19 20/0

Printed in the U.S.A.   40

First Scholastic printing, January 2015

Design by Ellen Huber
Art direction by Rita Marshall

Photographs by 123rf (cbpix), Alamy (Stephen Frink Collection), Dreamstime (Vladislav Gajic), Getty Images (Todd Bretl Photography), iStockphoto (Chris Dascher), Shutterstock (Rich Carey, cbpix, Fotokon, KKulikov, fluke samed, stockpix4u, Dray van Beeck), SuperStock (Mike Agliolo, Minden Pictures, Norbert Wu)

TABLE OF CONTENTS

Hello, sharks!

Sharks are big fish.

They live in
the oceans.

Sharks
have sharp,
pointy teeth.
They have
strong jaws.

Sharks have fins and a tail.

A shark's
skin is rough.
It feels like
sandpaper.

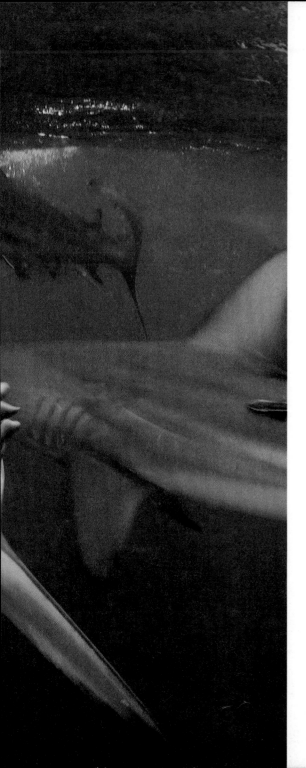

Most sharks
eat meat. They
eat fish and
other ocean
animals.

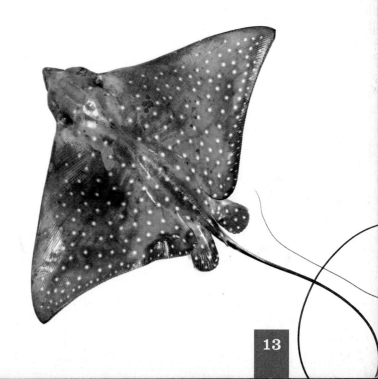

A baby shark is called a pup. A pup usually grows up by itself.

But some sharks live together in schools.

Sharks swim
through the ocean.

They look for food.

Goodbye, sharks!

Picture a Shark

gills

eye

snout

mouth

nostril

teeth

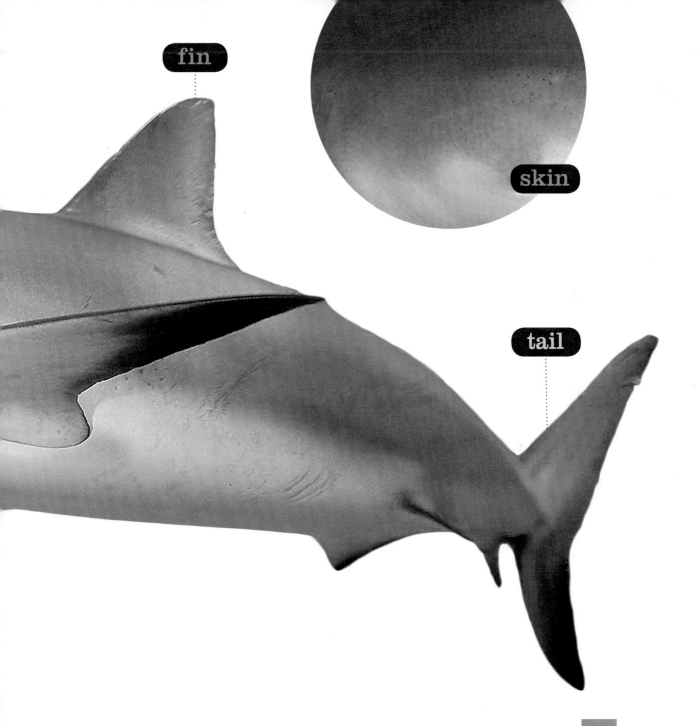

fin

skin

tail

Words to Know

fins: parts of a fish's body used for swimming

jaws: the upper and lower parts of the mouth

oceans: big areas of deep, salty water

schools: groups of fish, like sharks

Read More

Clarke, Ginjer. *Sharks!*
New York: Grosset & Dunlap, 2001.

Simon, Seymour. *Incredible Sharks.*
San Francisco: Chronicle Books, 2004.

Websites

Shark Activities
http://www.kidzone.ws/sharks/activities/index.html
Print out shark games or sheets to color. Put together
a puzzle online!

Sharks in the Classroom
http://www.enchantedlearning.com/subjects/sharks/
classroom/Classroomweblinks.shtm
Keep learning about sharks, with the help of fun activities.

Index